Printed by George Pulman & Sons, Watling Street, Bletchley, Bucks.

MOTORING THROUGH

edited by

Russell Brockbank

PUBLISHER: David & Charles: Newton Abbot
in association with PUNCH

Acknowledgements

Thanks are due to Marilyn Lawes and
Kate Chapman for their assistance in the
preparation of this book.
Some extracts from "You Have Been
Warned" have been included and thanks are
due to the publishers, Methuen & Co. Ltd.,
for permission to do so – to Mrs Kenneth Bird
for allowing the use of some of the Fougasse
contributions and to Donald McCullough
for the use of some of his contributions.

Introduction

Any new invention is a godsend to the derisive cartoonist because it gives him a fresh peg for displaying the follies of man. The arrival of a completely new form of transport in a country notorious for disliking change, let alone upheaval, was bad enough. But, when it menaced the sacred horse *and* was German in origin, it must have seemed the greatest threat to Britain since Napoleon's possible invasion.

Faced with the Automobile in 3-D the "Punch" editors could not ignore it. They represented the Establishment of the time and were expected to defend it, yet the people who were bringing in the contraptions were Establishment also. It thus became a struggle between those who ran down the foxes versus those who were beginning to run down the pedestrians. The opening pages of this book clearly show where the magazine's sympathies lay.

The "Punch" artists (only the weekly political drawing was called a "cartoon" in those days) stirred up the trouble as best they could. Those who had never been able to draw convincing horses – and had long envied those who could – fell upon the automobile with all the enthusiasm of the uncommitted, i.e. those who could not afford to own or drive either. Their first efforts clearly show their reluctance to get involved with machinery (there was a lot of deep shadow fudging the tricky entrails beneath the coachwork) but they could recognise a golden opportunity when they saw one. They sniped at both factions from the side-lines, snobbery being the main target.

One can feel sorry for the horse lovers. For centuries landowners had bred horses, dealers had sold them, harness makers had equipped them, grain merchants had helped feed them and coach makers had supplied the vehicles. There was in fact a vested interest in the animal when the automobile began shooting along the quiet lanes of the English countryside enclosed in a travelling duststorm. Taking their cue from the landed gentry, there was from the start a widespread resentment from the general public and the police; the former were outraged by the noise the cars made ("barks like a dog, stinks like a cat") and the dust they raised, while the latter prosecuted the drivers for exceeding 20 miles per hour – the pace of a carriage and pair. Speed traps proliferated, the police constantly varying the timed sections from one stretch of road to another. The "Motor Fiends" formed clubs in their own defence; hiring peasants, providing them with bicycles, distinctive armbands and binoculars, and sending them into the country to flush out the police and then advise the drivers. The police riposted by taking both scouts and drivers to court for obstructing the police in the execution of their duties. Not to be outdone the Automobile Association issued members' cars with distinctive badges and instructed the scouts *not* to salute the car when danger lay ahead; it was illegal to warn without stopping but perfectly legal for the driver to stop and ask the scout why he hadn't saluted. All very childish, but seventy years later this Hunter and Hunted relationship remains much the same, with radar in place of one policeman waving a hanky to another with a stopwatch a measured distance away.

The bookshop browser casually riffling through these pages might well say to himself "It's about nothing but cars", and put it down, but I would suggest it is a deal more than that, rather a piece of social history – that only "Punch" could have provided – centred on a great invention of our times which for good or ill has revolutionised the lives of us all. On the good side it has brought happiness to countless millions by enlarging their horizons, easing social intercourse – particularly with people of other nations – and improved the rapid exchange of goods. On the debit side it has killed and maimed great numbers, desecrated huge areas of countryside and polluted the air we breathe. And we can't do without it.

What do these cartoons reveal? The first drawing in the book is, I suggest, gloriously funny – until one reflects on accident figures today; that the first motorists considered themselves Lords of Creation and it was clearly the duty of peasants to keep clear of them; that hardly a driver today hasn't repeated at some time what a Motor Fiend said in 1900 – the difference being that we say it in relief when we have *avoided* running someone down. It is hard to credit but 29 years later Bert Thomas was still littering the road with semi-reclining figures (*fully* reclining would have been too much), and one can't help but laugh today. One of his ever-present policemen says "You've dragged this man one hundred yards", and the lady driver replies, "But only at 30 miles per hour". And we laugh again. Basically we haven't changed – the Old Adam is still there, heaven help us.

Has the whole Car Thing been a ghastly mistake? Should Gottlieb Daimler have been dangled from a beam in his workshop in 1884 before he could invent the first one? And after him likewise Hammel, Leon Bollee, Lutzman, Benz, Lanchester, Stevens, Darracq, Napier, Cadillac, Rolls and Royce, as fast as they picked up a spanner? And especially Henry Ford?

If all the oil wells in the world had dried up decades ago, we should be driving about nowadays in cars powered by Steam, Electricity or Nuclear Power, in relative silence and clean air. What a blessing for all mankind – except, that is, for outdated hoodlums like myself who positively adore the clatter of overhead camshafts, the Wagnerian symphony from the exhaust as one slices through the gears, the smell of warm oil, the bite of good brakes before the screech of the tyres through the next corner, the arc of the rev. counter needle racing round the dial, the whistle of the wind, the low moans of one's wife crouching in embryonic posture under the dashboard...

Russell Brockbank.

THE PIONEERS

Motor Fiend: 'Why don't you get out of the way?'
Victim: 'What! are you coming back?'

BROTHERS IN ADVERSITY
Farmer: 'Pull up, you fool! the mare's bolting!'
Motorist: 'So's the car!'

A QUIET VILLAGE

THE RETORT COURTEOUS

Motorist (cheerfully – to fellow-guest in house-party): 'What luck? Killed anything?'
Angler (bitterly): 'No. Have you?'

A POLICE TRAP

'I say, Bill, We can't be going more than twenty miles an hour! What do you think?'

Alarmed Motorist (after collision): 'Are you hurt?'
Butcher Boy: 'Where's my kidneys?'

THE PASSING OF THE HORSE

Probable scene in the proximity of police trap, now that the practice of warning motorists has been declared illegal.

NOT TO BE CAUGHT
Motorist (whose motor has thrown elderly villager into horse-pond):
'Come along, my man. I'll take you home to get dry.'
Elderly Villager: 'No, yer don't! I've got yer number and 'ere I stays
till a hinderpendent witness comes along!'

'It's stopped rainin', mister.'

Constable (to motorist who has exceeded the speed limit): 'And I have my doubts about this being your first offence. Your face seems familiar to me.'

Policeman (to motorist, who having inadvertantly left his car in charge of an expert thief, has had his magneto stolen): 'Now Sir, Would you be prepared to swear that you had it when you arrived?'

Countryman (to policeman regulating traffic): 'Coom out o' t' way, lad. Thou'lt be run over!'

THE STOWAWAY

Inspecting Officer: 'Which is the most important nut on this lorry?'
Driver (ex Infantry): 'I am, Sir.'

Dear old lady (having a lift – her first motor ride – as chauffeur signals a turn):
'Look here, young man – You keep both hands on the wheel. I'll tell you when it begins to rain.'

Salesman: 'It is possible that it may interest you to know that our
car was driven up all the flights of steps at the Crystal Palace.'
Inquiring Visitor: 'Well – er – not much. You see, I live in a bungalow.'

THE COURSE OF TRUE LOVE

Guide: 'Ladies an' Gen'lemen, We are now passin' one o' the oldest
public-'ouses in the country.' Passenger: 'Wot for?'

Nervous Passenger: 'What's that queer sound?'
Irish Chauffeur: 'Tis the foot-brake, Sorr, Is out of order and the hand-brake won't work. But don't
be onaisy, Sorr – the hooter is all right.'

Driver: 'Don't forget – Case of Accident – or anything – We're only doin' fifteen, – Must tell police same tale.'

AT THE MOTOR SHOW

*Salesman (peeved by gratuitous criticism): 'No Sir. We do not claim
that our equipment is as complete as that given with the 'Flash Car',
Which, I understand, includes an A.B.C. for use in breakdowns!'*

THE BACKFIRE

*Salesman: 'And what kind of horn would you like, Sir? Do you
care for a good loud blast?' Haughty Customer: 'No, I want something that just sneers.'*

Wife (to husband making futile effort to start car):
'Try winding it the other way, darling.'

Passenger: 'I think the country round here is extraordinarily pretty.'
Speed Fiend: 'Is it? I must see it some day.'

Aunt (frigidly): 'Tell me, Hector, Is this an accident, or
merely another thing that the car can do?'

THE MAN WHO HAD A LITTLE WALLPAPER LEFT OVER

The First Psychadelic Car?

The Driver: 'What do you think of these little things?'
The Passenger: 'Make topping ash-trays.'

P.C.: 'You were doing forty miles an hour, Sir.'
Motorist (whispering): 'Make it seventy, I'm trying to sell him the thing.'

THE CROSS-ROAD PROBLEM IN HOMESHIRE HAS AT LAST BEEN SOLVED
BY THE ADOPTION OF THE WARP AND WOOF SYSTEM

The First Flyover?

(*'And what happens when you wish to turn left or right?'*)

Very Rich Man (after minor accident): 'Ah! I thought so – A distinct dent. Now the question arises: What make of car shall we have next?'

Lady (held up for scorching): 'I say, This is a ridiculous waste of time. I gave all the facts to a policeman ten minutes ago.'

Prospective Purchaser: 'What's she like on hills?'
Owner: 'Hills! Down 'em in a jiffy.'

'I can't come out yet, Dear: I'm washing the baby.'

Constable: 'What sort of car was it?'
Casualty: 'Bit late, ain't yer? There's bin two more over me since then.'

THE HELPING HAND

The Thirties and War-Time

This period was dominated by two great draughtsmen. No apology need be made for the number of Bert Thomas' drawings for he was far and away the funniest until he ran out of accidents, policemen and steam. Fortuitously for Punch, Fougasse took up where Thomas left off and in a miraculous way said in drawings everything that can ever be said for Man in Motorcar, including "Nobody cares what the driver does, provided he doesn't reverse". Toward the end of the era – faced with the near-certainty of war – young men who would soon be flying Spitfires and Hurricanes affected boredom with everything, cars included. Paul Crum's, "I believe this hill is supposed to be one-in-something" is typical.

Again fortuitously for Punch, mechanically-minded Rowland Emett emerged from nowhere to spin his spidery fantasies in a world of tanks and aircraft during the second world war.

With most of the cartoonists in uniform Fougasse (art editor) concocted a scheme whereby cartoonists serving in far away places sent rough ideas in pencil to Punch for him to farm out to those fortunates still at home to make the finished drawings. Both the man overseas and the man on the spot were paid at the finished rate, thus assuring the magazine of the continued loyalty of valuable contributors after the war had ended. In addition the scheme kept the cartoonist in uniform "in the groove" which is vital to his survival.

GOOD NIGHT

Taxi-Driver (avoiding collision): 'D'you want the 'ole ——— road to yourself?'
Damsel: 'I've as much ——— right to the ——— road as you have.'
Taxi-Driver: 'Beg pardon, Lady.'

'Sound yer 'orn!' 'Sound your aitches!'

Father: 'What do you want a new car for? You've only had this a month.'
Daughter: 'Yes – but it's known to the police by now.'

Constable (suspiciously): 'Let me see your licence.'
Flapper: 'This is where you get stung. I'm too young to have one.'

Brother: 'Easy' Sis – you nearly swerved into her. What made you do that?'
Sister: 'I wanted a good look at her hat.'

'Why can't you remember to turn the wireless off when you leave the car, Henry?'

(First car radio cartoon)

Niece: 'No I never worry about the speedometer. I just go by the coppers' faces.'

Wife (bitterly): 'Why not buy *this* horse? He's the best we've had yet.'

'Haven't the foggiest idea what's wrong – But George always lifts this thing.'

Old offender: 'I say, ain't you goin' to read the minutes of the last meetin'?'

LE MOT JUSTE

'You dragged this man a hundred yards.'
'But only at thirty miles an hour.'

*Victim: 'You'll know the car all right. There's a
lady looking like this on the radiator.'*

Local Magistrate (angrily): 'Is this the first time you've been in trouble?'

Motorist (who is lost): 'Is this the road to St. Ives?'
Yokel: 'Dunno.'
Motorist: 'Is that the road to Willingham?'
Yokel: 'Dunno.'
Motorist: 'Well, can you tell me which is the road to Cottenham?'
Yokel: 'Dunno.'
Motorist (exasperated): 'Well, you don't seem to know much.'
Yokel: 'Maybe not; but I ain't lost.'

Owner of ancient car: 'Could you oblige me with a match?'
Owner of luxury car: 'Yes, but I shouldn't set fire to it here.'

CODE IN THE HEAD 1935

Before embarking on the road the novice should of course be familiar with the signals likely to be made by other drivers. So far as we know there is no book that gives anything like a complete list. The Highway Code, good as it is in every other way, prints examples, some of which are merely such as would be given by an experienced driver under ordinary circumstances. Thus they represent only a small proportion of the signals actually used, and, to the driver who wishes to know the meaning of the signals sent out by the car in front, they are not much good. We are therefore giving a version based upon the Highway Code, but with the additions that are nowadays essential.

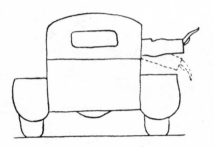

"I am going to slow down, or stop."

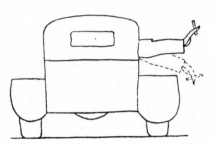

"I am going to shake the ash off my cigarette."

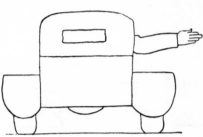

"I am going to turn to my right."

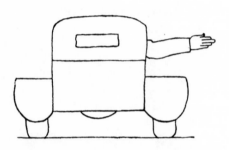

"I am going to turn to my right, and when I discover that it is the wrong turning I am going to turn back again just in time to give you the fright of your life."

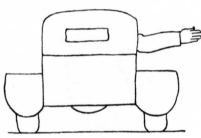

"Look, I can drive with one hand off the wheel."

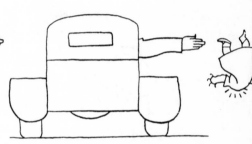

"By jove, there goes the baby."

"Take that you brute."

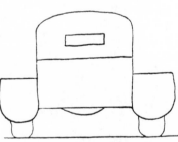

"I will not be overtaken."

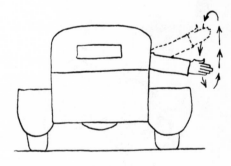

"I am going to turn left."

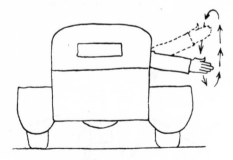

"My arms got pins and needles."

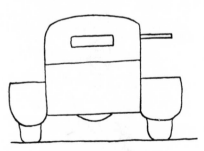

"I am going to the right"
or "I am going to stop"
or "I am going to slow down"
or "I am going to turn round"
or "See I press this thing and up it comes"

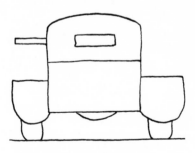

"I am going to turn left."

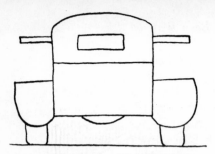

"I am going to have it put right tomorrow."

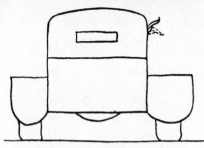

"I am going to turn to the left or the right or slow down or skid or stop or maybe dash across and ask the way from the policeman on point duty."

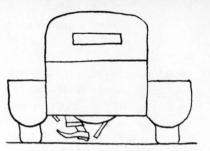

"I am going through the floor."

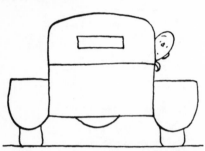

"I have just reversed into something."

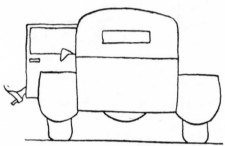

"I have just been insulted."

"I have just filled up with oil."

"I am going to keep well into the left side of the road."

"I am going to swerve suddenly out into the middle of the road and, with luck back again."

"I am going to appear suddenly from nowhere and dash straight across the road with a basket of groceries on my handle bars."

"I am going to remain on the carrier."

"I am not going to remain on the carrier."

"Run over me if you dare."

"Run over me if you like."

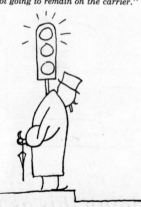

"I am going to wait till the light goes green and then step slowly off the pavement."

Cars must not remain in Official Parks for more than two hours at a stretch.
That is why we all come out of the theatre during the interval –

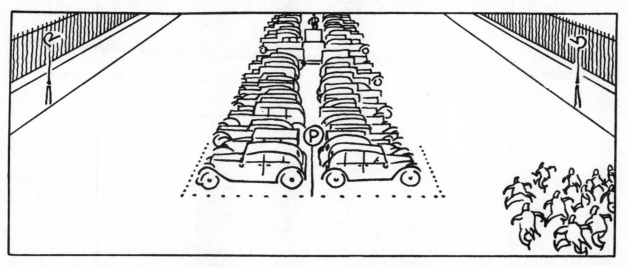

And move our cars carefully clear of their park –

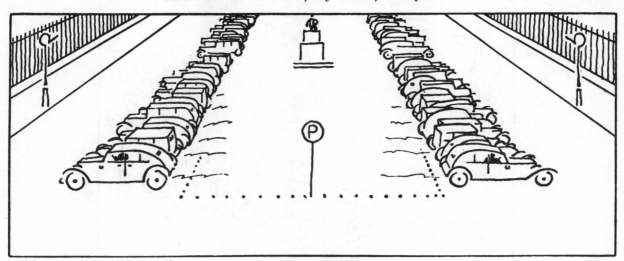

And back again into it –

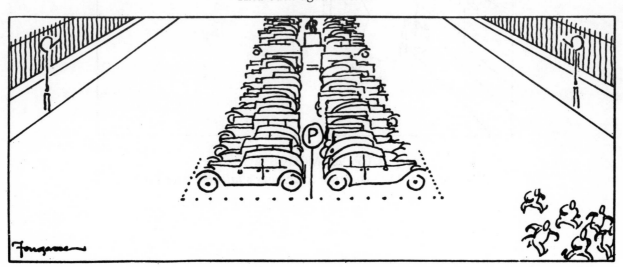

The joke being that this isn't a joke at all.

Were we really doing this as far back as 1936?

OUR VICARIOUS AGE

'By Gad, Sir, The insurance companies shall smart for this!'

One of the great truths

Nobody cares what the driver does –

provided he doesn't reverse!

And another . . .

THE FIRST SCRATCH—

AND THE LAST

...and another

'Did the Ramblers win all right?'

'No'

'I believe this hill is supposed to be one-in-something.'

'Yes dear, I'm boiling some water for the radiator –
and I'm heating up a tin of petrol for you too.'

'D'you mind switching off, Sir? She's gaining on me.'

'I forget the exact name of the village, but
you can't mistake it, because there's
a notice outside it saying thirty.'

'And do I have to keep on holding this?'

'Royal School of Needlework – and drive like mad.'

'No, Darling, I don't think it feels a bit as if we had a flat tyre.'

'One misses a lot not understanding the lingo.'

'It never fails to amaze me how these
taxi-drivers find their way about at night.'

'Taxi?'

'Right, there, in the distance, First a green, then an amber, then a red signal, and they keep on flashing one or two at a time.'

'I think you're very clever; I couldn't even draw a straight line.'

Trooper Doughty leaves to rejoin his Regiment, 1742.

506249 DOUGHTY S. D. gets back to barracks, 1942.

'They say, can we do two
hundred and eighty-seven
Dainty Afternoon Teas?'

'You people seem to forget there's specially bombed car-parks provided for the purpose.'

'It's all right – I expect they tell them that over here we drive on the left . . .'

Summertime . . . do you remember how we used to jump gaily into our cars and go off for –

a breather, how we used to roam about –

the countryside, along the little lanes and byways, enjoying –

the wind on the beach and the song of the birds and –

all the little wayside flowers –

with, maybe, a bathe in some secluded spot –

or, possibly, a ramble across the downs:

do you remember how we used to picnic far from the haunts of men –

and, perhaps, finish up by dining in some quaint little village inn?

Ah me, ah me, how different is today!

APRES LA GUERRE FINIS

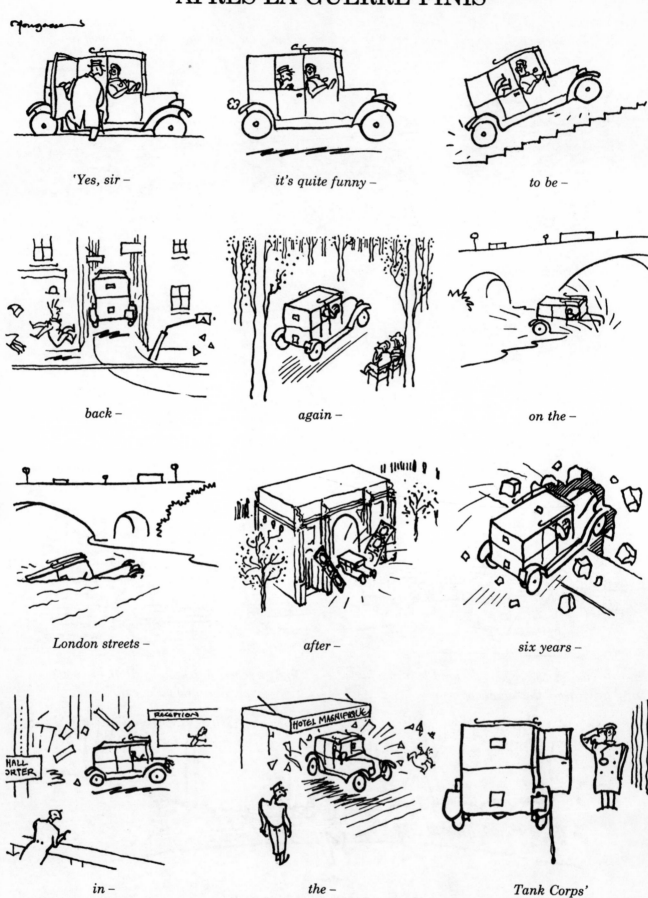

'Yes, sir –

it's quite funny –

to be –

back –

again –

on the –

London streets –

after –

six years –

in –

the –

Tank Corps'

Post-war Forties

Taking considerably longer to get out of uniform than to get into it, the ex-warrior cartoonists were late in picking up the threads of a civil life burdened by food rationing and shortages of almost everything. This section is brief because cars were in short supply and petrol was rationed. One gets ideas about cars if one is driving cars, but these few drawings show considerable joie de vivre.

'It's my wife – but there's probably some quite simple explanation.'

'There should be some terrific car parks if they use the atom bomb.'

'No, same old car . . . new engine . . .'

'Better vowels than the last one, so we're
heading West all right.'

'Sometimes I rather wish we hadn't expanded into a quintet.'

'And <u>that's</u> said to be the most painted village in England.'

The Fifties

This period produced something of a flood of motoring cartoons, possibly because the artists had realized that Fougasse (now editor) and Brockbank (art editor) were car-crazy, and fed them accordingly. Even when Malcolm Muggeridge succeeded Fougasse and politics took precedence over all else – the art editor was able to keep up the flow thanks to Langdon, Smilby, Burgin, Starke, Graham, Thelwell and three eminent Frenchmen – André François, Sempe and Bosc. Larry's motoring ideas have to be seen to be believed; he sold thirty to Punch in one day – which isn't to say he *drew* thirty in that time, but he might have.

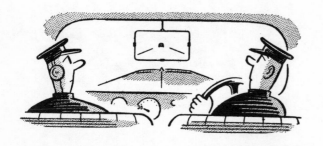

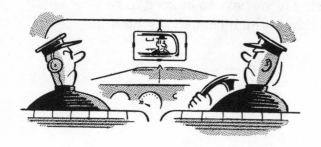

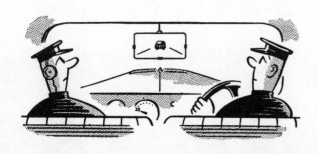

'No, no, no! Bless my soul! On yer other lock, left, and well down. Blimey, if only _I_ could drive . . .'

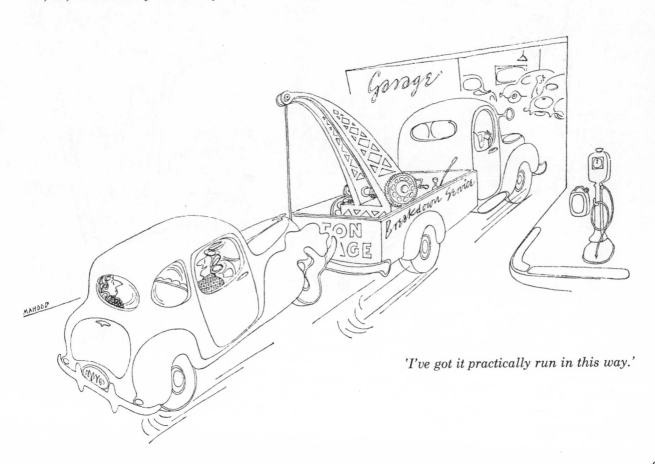

'I've got it practically run in this way.'

'There, what did I say? I arrive here every day at 10.12 a.m. precisely,
and precisely at 10.12 a.m. every day he slams the thing shut in my face.'

'There's the *first* lie – the booklet said it would cruise happily at sixty all day.'

There's one thing I'm absolutely determined about:

the next car I buy –

is going to be –

one –

that's –

very much –

easier –

to get –

in and out of.

'Now this is just the sort of thing that
does not help Anglo-American relations . . .'

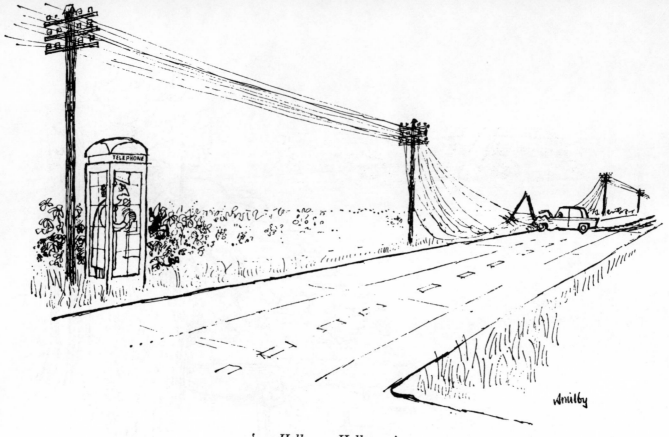

'...Hello...Hello...'

'Don't just lie there, stupid. Do something!'

'I'll take that one.'

'There goes a car with exactly the same number as ours.'

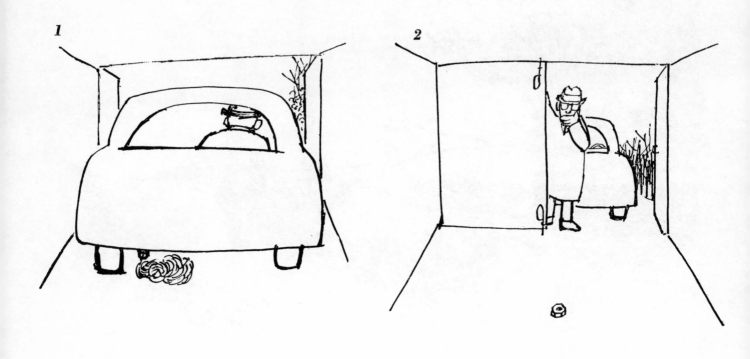

3

4

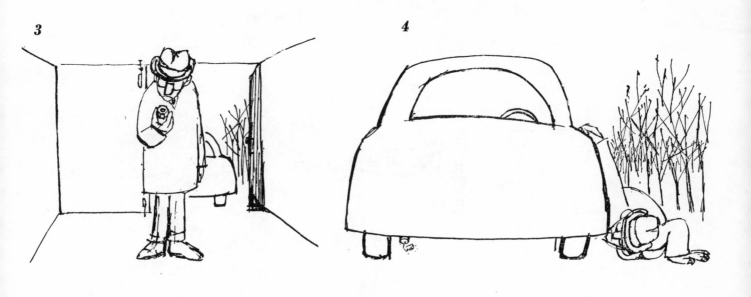

7

8

André Francois

'I wouldn't want a new car, Hilda – I'd be afraid of every blessed scratch.'

'The zipper's jammed.'

'We'll have to stop meeting like this. My insurance company's getting suspicious.'

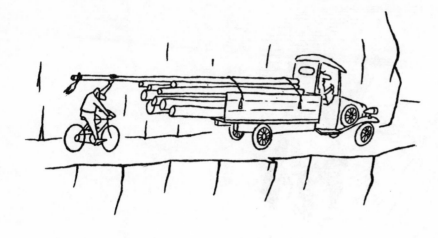

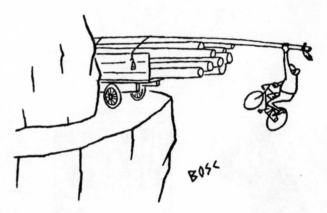

'She keeps making supersonic bangs.'

'Straight on be quicker, but t'other be prettier.'

'It's a strange sort of noise – rather like hair-pins being dropped into a plastic tea-cup.'

'I bet you neither of us has got any —   — change.'

'Why it's easy!'

'No, no, Mrs. Williams . . .

I'm afraid you'll have to go back . . .

and do it again . . .'

'*A perfect example, I'd say of the money getting in the wrong hands*'.

'They're not the street cries I knew as a gel!'

'I'm being served, thank you.'

'I'm all ruddy thumbs
to-day. Took me
over five seconds to
change that wheel.'

'Keep your eye on that oil temperature – watch that rev counter – mind that four-wheel drift.'

The Sixties

By this time a new editor (whose antipathy to machinery was profound) and a new art editor had got the paper back on an even keel, to the point where Punch was no longer in danger of being stacked on bookstalls with the rest of the motoring press. Full page drawings and the Frenchmen practically disappeared in favour of strips and "smalls" and Bill Hewison produced a classic on a man pumping up a flat tyre. As cars became so like one another, it is hardly surprising that the artist gave up identifying them. Burgin unhappily died in his prime – a great loss to the paper – and Holland, Albert, Williams and Dickinson arrived.

'Well, really!'

'There are plenty of parking spaces if you know where to look for them.'

'No more for Henry, thank you, he's got to remember where we've parked the car.'

'Back up a bit, dear, and see how it looks.'

'And what's this item – to checking service costs, adjusting addition and eliminating overcharge, one pound five shillings?'

'All ready for you, Mr. Milligan.'

RELIGIOUS REVIVAL

'The Steeple Fund was over-subscribed.'

'Excuse me – if there is any forgiving to be done it is going to be done by me.'

'They could perfectly well have gone round by Quarry Hill!'

'For once I don't feel my ears burning.'

'Now unscrew the two bolts securing the induction manifold,
and remove the float valve needle from the seating . . .'

'Thank you, sir. I must say, give me my old motor cycle combination any day.'

'Most of those millions of teeming, crawling ants you refer to, mate,
bring us in a 3 guinea a year subscription . . . Over.'

MASCOTS

by McLACHLAN

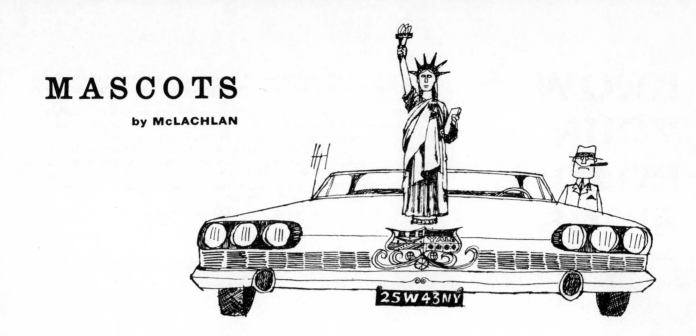

KNOW YOUR ROAD SIGNS

Thanks to our educational system it has—up to now—been safe to assume that any Briton who could afford a car could read, and our road signs warned, ordered or advised us in the mother tongue.

It is generally agreed that education on the Continent lags far behind our own, but not until one first drives on their roads does one realise that their drivers only understand the sort of primitive symbols we associate with Emergent Africans going to the polls.

OK then, chacun son gout, but why inflict them on a "higher" civilisation like OURS?

If we have a weakness, it is our lack of enthusiasm for the graphic arts. We never have (and probably never will) understood what the artist was driving at: admitting this, how downright dangerous it is to face us with cabalistic signs needing instant understanding and prompt action—even at only seventy mph from now on!

It should be admitted that we foisted this one ⊘ on to the Continent some years back, and in our present difficulty we can only hope they are in the same confusion over whether it means twenty past ten o'clock or ten minutes to four.

- -

Face to face with the list of these things—in a booklet the authorities *don't* send us—we find . . .

No Riderless
Bicycles Allowed

No Eel Fishing
Allowed On
The Clearway

Steep Hill Upwards
(or is it Downwards?)

Hardly Noticeable
Hill Downwards
(or is it Upwards?)

Disintegrating
Lorry Ahead

- -

Beware of
Low-Flying
Motorcycles

Roadmen
Sawing Down Trees

Roadmen
Sawing Up Logs

Is Your
Steering Wheel
Done Up Properly?

Sophia Loren
Ahead

- -

Water Diviner
Ahead

Outdoor Pop Art
Display

Veteran Locomotive
Rally On The Move

Unusual Roadman
Ahead

?

'If they can't make up their minds
how can they expect a nit like you to?'

'When did we last have
the parlor chimney swept?'

'I'd give a lot to know
which adjective they've censored out?'

'Why can't they get their symbols more like real life?'

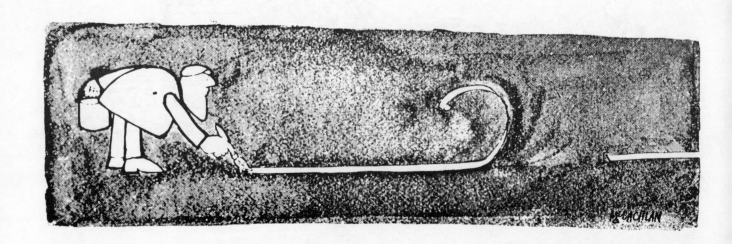

COME RAIN, COME SHINE

'And now we've got a slow puncture.'

'I shouldn't worry about it. It can't last much longer.'

DUMPING

'I've got a three-litre Rover at the moment – about a mile outside Salford.'

'There's a space, Dad!'

'Don't dump yours there – we'll be double dumped!'

'Hullo! It's started.'

BREAKING

'We've offered him alternative accommodation.'

'Fred – that black Wolseley with the light on top.'

'Damn cheek! Someone's abandoned an old car right on our doorstep!'

'Fiat 500, E-Type Jag, Hillman Husky, Austin Mini Cooper S., Aston Martin DB4 . . .'

'You're OK, but I'm having him down at the station.'

'Ho-ho! Who's been watering the damn beer then?'

Man in
Motor Car
by LARRY

COPS...

'Stop worrying. She told me she'd leave
a car for us round the corner.'

'... and of course you'll have the added advantage of being able to
sneak in below radar level.'

'Sounds rather like fun, dear, having a little round label sort of thing, stuck on about here, different colour each four months.'

'. . . stolen . . . registration number PGX 890, Two door Anglia. Arabesque motif over bonnet and roof in purple, pink and turquoise. Paisley pattern sidepanels in lavender, emerald and peacock blue.'

...AND ROBBERS

'You chaps going to be long?'

'Daily Globe! There's been a six-vehicle pile up in Maple Road!'

'What with one thing and another the only use we have for the car nowadays is
that it stops other people from nicking our place.'

'How was I to know what he meant by 'puddie mocar'?'

'Aren't you out of bed yet?'

AND A WHIFF OF THE SEVENTIES...

'I might have known! A bloody woman driver!'

'Thanks for the lift – it's a battered old can but it gets me there and brings me back.'

'I'm worried about Charlie. The boot hasn't been slept in.'

'The tourist trade means a lot to the town's economy, sir.'

'This is extremely kind of you, sir. Can I interest you in becoming a member?'

Tenez á Droite

No book on this subject would be complete without a section on driving on the "wrong" side of the road. That the British set off for the Continent in hundreds of thousands of cars each summer is a remarkable act of bravery; that most of them return relatively unscathed is nothing short of a miracle. Almost all are convinced that by speaking English loudly and slowly they will be understood anywhere. When this fails they are reduced to drawing with an index finger on the dusty sides of the car, or pointing at the object of their desire. Some actually pick up a phrase or two which will have been forgotten by the time they cross the channel the following year. When driven almost out of their minds by the stupidity of foreigners they take sanctuary in Switzerland where everybody (on main roads) speaks English. Comparatively few foreigners bring their cars to Britain more than once. Chesterton was right in saying "The rolling English drunkard made the rolling English road".

'Ah well, bang goes the Concours d'Elégance.'

'Shouldn't it be in French?'

'Now we'll see just what the Premier Garage,
High Street, Little Primley, means by 'check and
adjust brakes, one pound five shillings and sixpence'.'

'I didn't even know we'd played them in the World Cup.'

'No, I think he's all right to ask the way. It's the chaps in round black helmets
who knock your teeth in.'

'Congratulations, Lady Pamela. You have bagged your first lion!'

PACKAGE

SAFARI

by

LARRY

'Henry! Do please remember there's no reciprocal free health treatment here.'

'What the hell's that supposed to mean?'

First day of the 'No Hooting' rule in Paris.

'Cinq francs supplément, s'il vous plait.'

'Malheureusement mon mari a tué un de vos canards.'

Roadhogmanay

Of course most of the trouble on the road would be
avoided if people would only cultivate a sense of proportion
and stop driving much too fast in the hopes of saving five
minutes that they don't know what to do with when they've
saved them and then they would be able to drive a perfectly
beautiful machine along a perfectly wonderful road in perfect
peace and toleration as I'm doing now instead of thinking
they've got to roar about and hoot and risk every one's lives
by cutting in like that fellow in the blue car in front which
only makes them get into a filthy state of nerves over anything
likely to hinder their foul progress like that madman who's just
passed and if they only realized it they'd get there just as
quickly and easily if they took it perfectly calmly as I'm doing
or anyhow they would if only the ridiculous way they go on didn't
hinder every one else like this blithering idiot who's just
turned right across us and if half-baked louts like this man just
in front didn't glue themselves to the crown of the road and make
one hoot at them till one's completely deaf and if half-witted
pedestrians like that one didn't simply hurl themselves under the
wheels whenever one appeared suddenly round a bend, and if this
type of lorry-driving fiend didn't lumber about the roads
hiding everything in front so that one has just got to trust
blindly to luck every time one cuts in front of them on a
corner and if absolute raving lunatics like this one didn't
hurtle at full speed along a main road quite oblivious of the
fact that we might be dashing suddenly out of a side road at
the same moment and if everything else on the road didn't take
a perfectly hellish delight in getting in one's way and making
one lose precious minutes and blast you will you get out of my –
CRASH TWANG TINKLE BUMP . . . !

from "You Have Been Warned" Fougasse & McCullough (1935)

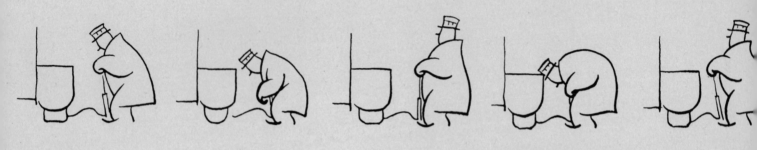